Beautifully Scarred

A STORY OF A MOTHER'S RESILIENCE, FAITH, AND
UNWILLINGNESS TO LET HER BABY DIE.

CEWANDA TODD

Mary

9.19.19

Thank you for your support. May your faith be restored

Cewanda Todd

ISBN 13: 978-1-79-021099-2

Printed in the United States of America

CONTENTS

ACKNOWLEDGEMENTS

Damon, we endured some hard stuff. Thank you loving me through those days when I was just sad and there was nothing you could do or say to make me better. There is no other man that I would have rather gone through this with. Kendall is so blessed to call you dad.

Sydney, I could not have gotten through many days if you were not such a responsible young lady. I never wanted you to feel unloved or ignored when I had to give so much of me to your sister. Thank you for never making me feel like I loved her more. I felt guilty when I was with her and not you, with you and not her. I love you more than you know.

Quentin, you are the best son and big brother ever. You may not have understood all the things that were happening around you and you got shuffled around a lot. Thank you for not complaining and saying "What about me?" You were never selfish or complained when we couldn't be with you for long periods of time. The bond that you have with your sister now makes me smile. Thank you for being her protector.

Dianna (mom), I cannot thank you enough for all the things you did during these past few years. If we did not have you to depend on, I don't know what we would have done. You are the most loyal, giving, kindhearted, selfless person I know. You took care of Quentin, cleaned my house, cooked food, and visited the hospital, time and time again. Even when I wanted to be alone you were there because you said, "The same way you are here for your baby I will be here for you." Even still, you are the one I can always count on.

Detroit's Children's Hospital of MI, everyone that we have come into contact with and has taken care of Kendall over the years, thank you. I cannot mention all of you by name but please know that we extend our greatest thanks to you for the work that you do everyday.

Krissy Richards (PA), the Drs. and nurses told me you called on your days off and checked on Kendall. Many days you shared stories with me about your sons health challenges and it gave me hope.

Janet Mcgiver (NP), from the first day in Dr Delius' office before Kendall was born until the day you had to tell us "they're doing everything they can do" you have always been there for us or a phone call away.

Colette Squire, thank you for being my confidante, cardiac nurse extraordinaire. From the 1st day of the 2nd open-heart surgery we became much more than your patients' mom. You became our family. Thank you for making sure I ate, always bringing me coffee and embarrassing me and having the EMS come to Kendall's room to pick me up on a stretcher, push me through the hallways and tunnel to another hospital to get treatment on myself because I was dehydrated and weak but refused to go to the hospital on my own. Thank you for being my friend even now

Dr. Daniel Turner, we started off with a different cardiologist who kept saying Kendall would die and was so negative. Thank you for agreeing to put your commitment to your colleague aside and agree to be her doctor. You have been a godsend for our family. Your compassion, commitment and love for cardiac kids makes me so relieved that you are her doctor.

Cathy Farris, you are the one who recognized something was wrong with Kendall. The only way to know that was to know her. You'd taken care of her so many times that you knew there was a change in her condition. I will forever be grateful to you that you were her nurse on December 20th.

Dr. Ralph Delius, you are a brilliant surgeon. I know for sure God used your brilliant mind and your skillful hands to perform your best work on my baby countless times. You always gave us hope and I truly believe she was your favorite patient. God saved her life but He used your skilled hands as the instrument.

Dr. Patrick Hines, I will forever be grateful for you. Thank you for not giving up, for not stopping the code blue. Another doctor probably would have. Thank you for listening to your heart and saving her like she was your own child. Thank you for always treating her like she was your family and not just another patient

Pastor Andrea Ellis and members of Destiny Faith Church, and to all of our family, friends, co-workers, teachers and even complete strangers: your prayers, encouragements, meals, money and phone calls allowed us to stay encouraged, feel loved, supported, cared about and covered in prayer. Because of your help we have been empowered to "fight the good fight of faith" and continue to believe in the promises of God. We appreciate and love all of you. God bless you.

To all of the mothers who are informed of a diagnosis either before or after delivery, you will go through a range of emotions, maybe even feel like you cannot do it. I had depression, anxiety, insomnia, highs and lows, happiness and sadness, but you don't have to suffer alone. Together we will support each other through the good and the bad, together. We do not have to suffer in silence because we don't want to "bother" our loved ones or feel like no one understands, or we don't want anyone to know how scared we really are, or feeling like you are a ball of emotions all of the time. Please know that you are stronger than you think. God would have not placed this precious baby in your hands if He didn't already know that YOU are exactly who this child needed. He loves us that much to trust us with this gift.

Beautifully Scarred

A STORY OF A MOTHER'S RESILIENCE, FAITH, AND
UNWILLINGNESS TO LET HER BABY DIE.

CEWANDA TODD

CHAPTER 1

THE DIAGNOSIS

[T]hat your days and the days of your children may be multiplied in the land that the Lord swore to your fathers to give them, as long as the heavens are above the earth.

Deuteronomy 11:21

When I met my husband in 2001, I had a seven-year-old daughter, Sydney, from a previous relationship. We were married in 2005 and had two children together. Quentin is our son and our daughter's name is Kendall. This book is primarily written to focus on Kendall, our youngest child. We decided we wanted a third, and final, child and I got pregnant with Kendall in 2008. At that time, I was 38 years old.

It was a good time in our lives. We were financially, emotionally and physically prepared for this new addition to our family. We both had stable, secure jobs. My husband was, and still is, in the Air Force. I am a Registered Nurse.

At that time, our two kids were fourteen and four years old. We were happy and excited because we wanted this baby. We were both working full-time. Both children were in school. Everybody was healthy and we didn't have any issues. Life was good.

I had high blood pressure during my pregnancy with Quentin, which never went back to normal after the pregnancy.

So, I was diagnosed with chronic hypertension and I have been on blood pressure medication since 2005. With the exception of high blood pressure and a history of migraines, I was pretty healthy. My blood pressure over the years was under control as long as I was on the medication. So, the pregnancy didn't cause my blood pressure to go any higher.

I am an OB nurse, which means I take care of pregnant girls and women all of the time. At the time when I became pregnant with Kendall, I had worked in OB for fourteen years. I worked at the same hospital that I was going to deliver my baby. I knew all the OB doctors and ultrasound techs. Since I was an OB nurse, and already had two healthy children, I expected this pregnancy to be perfect, with no complications. Besides, people always say that each pregnancy is easier. They're wrong. At 19 weeks, I had my first ultrasound. My husband and I were excited to see our baby for the first time, but we kept turning our heads from the screen because we didn't want to know the sex. I have been in plenty of delivery rooms and ultrasound appointments with my patients—enough to know when something is not right. You can read it in the eyes of doctors and technicians without them saying a word. I knew that "look." So when the technician said, "Let me go get the doctor so he can take a look," I knew there was something wrong.

As the ultrasound tech pointed to the screen, the doctor was looking at the baby, nodding his head to whatever they were whispering about. That's when he said, "The baby has an abnormality in its heart. It's too early to see exactly what's wrong, so I need you to come back in two weeks when you are twenty-one weeks. We will take another look and do an Echo (ultrasound of the baby's heart)."

When we returned in two weeks for an Echo, our baby was diagnosed with congenital heart disease. Hypoplastic Right Heart Syndrome (HRHS) was the official diagnosis, which means the right ventricle was not developed. Our baby's heart had three chambers instead of four. The baby also had pulmonary atresia and tricuspid valve atresia. The left ventricle was fine, which pumps blood through your body. The missing right ventricle is the one that would have pumped blood to the lungs.

Doctors told us the prognosis wasn't good, and that usually these children didn't do well nor live long.

We were given three options. We could continue the pregnancy, have the baby and, if the pulmonary artery wasn't too small, the doctor would be able to perform surgery. If the pulmonary artery wasn't large enough, surgery would not be done and the baby would die. Our second option was to let the baby die in the hospital, or simply take it home to die. Our final option was to have an abortion ASAP. I was so overcome with grief that day. Over the next few days, I was in a daze. The abortion was not an option. I felt my baby kick and move. We already had a bond. How could I justify aborting my baby because I didn't get a "normal" one?

I was no longer happy about the pregnancy. My joy was completely ripped away from me. How would I be able to carry a baby for four more months, only to let it be born to die? Because of the apparently inevitable outcome, I didn't want to get attached to "it." Every couple of weeks, I had another Echo, hoping and praying a miraculous right ventricle had grown and everything was going to be alright. But instead, each time, we were told the baby was growing, but the lung artery was not.

Instead of the remaining months being a time of celebration and anticipation, it was a period of grieving. Grief over the loss of my dreams for the pregnancy. Grief over the loss of my dreams for the baby. Grief over the fact that the baby wouldn't have a life. To say I was devastated would be an understatement.

At thirty-five weeks, I had to decide where I was going to deliver the baby. I could deliver at the hospital where I worked, but the baby would be transferred to Children's Hospital in Detroit where the open heart surgery would be performed. This meant that I would be separated from my baby for a couple of days until I was discharged from the hospital. My other option was to deliver at the hospital that is connected to Children's Hospital, where the baby would be going for surgery immediately. This would mean I'd have to find a new doctor to deliver my baby. I was torn because I really wanted my own doctor, who had been my doctor for fourteen years, to deliver my baby. But I felt like I needed to deliver at the hospital closer to the Children's Hospital where the baby was going to be after birth. We did not buy any baby items, decorate the room nor have a baby shower. I couldn't bear the thought of preparing all of these things and never being able to bring my baby home. I saw my new doctor four times over the last four weeks of my pregnancy.

On April 17, 2009, my husband and I went to lunch, then decided to go shopping to pass some time before we had to pick our son up from school. During our shopping excursion, my water broke. We headed down to the hospital. I was quiet on the forty- minute drive to the hospital because I didn't know what was going to happen to this baby after it was born. I knew as long as I was pregnant, the baby was okay because it was getting all of its blood supply and oxygen from me. Once the baby was born, it was going to be hooked up to all kinds of machines, oxygen and medications to keep it alive. Kendall Jordyn Todd was born on April 17, 2009, at 11:21 p.m., weighing 6 pounds, 10.7 ounces.

I could hear her crying in the intensive care unit.

Usually, when you hear your baby cry for the first time, you cry tears of joy. I was crying tears of sorrow and grief because I didn't know if they would be able to do surgery on her. Even if they were able, would she survive the procedure? They took her to Children's Hospital in a mini ambulance. I had to wait three hours before I could see her. When I finally did get to see her, all the time in the world could not have prepared me for what I saw. All of those tubes, machines and IV's was overwhelming, to say the least.

To make matters worse, once I was discharged from the hospital, I had to go home. I remember the Sunday they handed me my discharge papers at 4 p.m. My plan was to go home and spend time with my other two children, get a good night's sleep, and return the next morning to the hospital for the surgery. I cried all the way home. I felt sick. How could I leave her behind, even if it was only for a few hours? What if something happened to her while I was at home? I jumped every time my phone rang. I didn't know how to go home, eat dinner and have casual conversation with my family, knowing what we would face the next day. I couldn't stay home. I just had to see Kendall again that same night. So, at 10 p.m., we drove back to the hospital so I could look at her and hold her hand.

On the fourth day of her life, she had her first open heart surgery. HRHS is a very rare congenital heart condition. It is a condition in which the right ventricle in the heart is underdeveloped. It causes inadequate blood flow to the lungs and causes the baby to be blue. HRHS in itself is rare, but congenital heart disease is the most common birth defect and can occur in 1/110 births. We were fortunate enough to have it detected prior to her birth so that we could be prepared medically.

The first scheduled surgery was called the Hemi-Fontan. As with any open heart surgery, doctors make an incision down the center of the chest.

The surgeons have to crack open the breastbone in order to have direct access to the heart in order to repair it.

Kendall had to be placed on a heart lung bypass machine during this time. The surgeries that Kendall had were the Hemi-Fontan (twice) and Fontan procedures. This is one of the types of operations for children born with a single ventricle. It is done in stages, spread out over the first few years of life. It is complicated and not easy to explain, but the purpose is to reduce the volume of work of the single ventricle. She has the left ventricle, which pumps blood to the body. But she was not born with the right ventricle, which pumps blood to the lungs. As a result, one of her lungs is smaller than the other. She's had several shunts placed in attempt to create a connection between her aorta and pulmonary artery. This is a temporary way to deliver blood to the lungs. Each and every one of the shunts they put in surgically, clotted and did not work. As a matter of fact, the first one that clotted caused her to need emergency surgery after two weeks to save her life. So, instead of three scheduled open heart surgeries, she had three scheduled and one emergency.

The first surgery went well. She was discharged home after two weeks. Some of the things the nurses told me that would be normal for her would be: a bluish color around the mouth, oxygen levels between 75-85% and exhaustion after crying. She was home for approximately one week. It was the first day my husband went back to work. My oldest daughter went to school. I dropped my son off at preschool. In the car on the way home, Kendall wouldn't stop crying. We got back home and she was still crying. She cried for twenty minutes. After she stopped crying, she was lethargic and pale. She looked really tired. Since this was part of the normal stuff they said would happen, I just held her and watched her. And watched her. And watched her. I needed reassurance that she was okay. She was breathing normally, but my gut was telling me something was not right. I just held her and rocked her...and cried. This was my first time alone with her and I was starting to go into panic mode. I didn't want to be one of those hypochondriacal parents who took their kid to ER all the time and nothing was wrong.

I just couldn't get rid of that sickening feeling that I had that something was wrong. I wanted her to give me a sign that she was okay.

I called my husband, who came home so we could take her back to the hospital. By the time we hit the freeway, I was in the back seat with her, crying and praying. At that point, it didn't matter to me that neither one of us was wearing a seatbelt. I couldn't put her down. I knew that was the last time I was going to hold her alive. I was panicking. Yelling to him to drive faster. She wasn't having trouble breathing at all. She looked peaceful. She looked like she was leaving me. You're probably wondering why I didn't call 911. Surely, I would have if she was not breathing or didn't have a heartbeat. That wasn't the case. All I kept remembering was that she had so many conditions that a local hospital wouldn't be able to help her. I didn't want to waste any time going in the wrong direction. I knew she couldn't tolerate a lot of oxygen at one time, and the first thing EMS would do was place a mask on her face. She wouldn't be able to tolerate it, but they wouldn't understand that. I had to get her where they could help her. That trip to the hospital that would've taken us 40 minutes with the posted speed limit took us approximately 15 minutes because we were on a mission to save her life.

As soon as we got through the emergency room doors, they grabbed her from me and quickly called code blue. I was having an out-of-body experience. This was not happening. I lost count of the people who were around her bed. They moved us over to a wall. The next thing I remember was a chaplain standing next to me. I felt my legs giving out on me, but I couldn't fall because, at that point, I couldn't even move. I was catatonic. There were people coming from everywhere, from every department, to work on Kendall. They told us they saw a clot in her shunt in her on the ultrasound. She had to be transported to the Cath Lab immediately to try to remove it.

Hours later, they told us they couldn't successfully remove the clot without opening her chest back up. They had to take her for what would be her second open- heart surgery in two weeks. Before they took her to surgery, there were all kinds of doctors and nurses in the room, pushing medication and blood through her IV.

Before they took her to surgery, they told me to tell her, "Goodbye." I knew what that meant. I saw the looks. It meant 'goodbye,' not 'see you later.' I couldn't say it. All I could say over and over was, "Don't leave me, Kendall. Please don't leave me!" If she died that day, I didn't know how I would live without her, or if I wanted to, for that matter.

CHAPTER 2

IN THE BEGINNING

Trust in the LORD with all your heart and lean not on your own understanding; in all your ways submit to him, and he will make your paths straight.

Proverbs 3:5-6

For what reasons did He choose to give Kendall to me? Why me? Out of all the women He could've chosen, why me? I never questioned why she was born with this defect, although I thought it. I was too scared to let such a question come out of my mouth because I've learned not to question God. But I have often thought I wasn't mentally strong enough to handle this. Surely, God knew I suffered from anxiety and panic attacks. He probably should've given her to somebody who smiled all the time and was never stressed out by day-to-day events.

People kept telling us, "God won't give you more than you can handle. God only gives children with special needs or challenges to the people whom He knows will take care of them the best." Huh? I didn't think I had what it took to do this temporarily, let alone a lifetime. But it's true. You never know what you can do until you *have* to do it. Until you're faced with the challenge, it's easy to say, "I can't do it." "I don't have it in me." "I'm not strong enough to handle all of this." It's easy to say you can't do something when the situation hasn't presented itself yet.

I used to say I would never be able to take care of a child with any type of physical disabilities, until I was put in a position to do it.

That supernatural strength comes when you need it to because you don't have time to think about *how* you're going to do it. You just start doing it. Then, you look back one day and say, "Wow, I didn't know I had it in me." If God entrusted me with this precious gift, He knew I had it in me to do it. I needed to know Him on a deeper level for who He really is. By Him giving me Kendall, I had to learn to trust and depend on Him in a different way. I had to trust Him because He trusted me with this child. I thought I knew God before Kendall, but I really didn't get to know His character until I had to call on Him for different aspects. I needed to know Him as a way maker, not just on the surface and for what He could do for me. Not for the jams

He could get me out of, or how He would bless me, even when I didn't acknowledge Him. A much deeper relationship was required.

Sometimes when you're going through a situation, you feel like this has never happened to anyone else. "Even if it has happened to someone else, it surely can't have been as devastating as my situation." That's how we tend to think. Surely, the details of what I'm going through trumps someone else's situation, right? When you receive devastating news, news that pulls the rug from underneath you, knocks the wind out of you, it is life-changing. Immediately, we go into saying, "I don't know what I'm going to do. This one's going to take me out." Your friends can listen, encourage and support you, but nobody can get you through something like this but God. You can call your mother, sister, brother, best friend, prayer partner or significant other. God is the only one who knows and understands what you need.

He had been waiting for me to need Him like this. This is exactly what He had been waiting for—for me to need, trust and depend on Him to keep me from falling. I always believed He would change other people's situations. I've cried with and for friends. Prayed with them and for them. But, what about me? Why was it so hard for me to believe those same prayers would save Kendall and me? I was, I am, brokenhearted. Devastated. Emotionally unstable. I wanted her fixed *now*. Immediately. Not years down the road. Right now. I wanted to look on the screen of all those heart catheterizations and ultrasounds and for one of the medical personnel to yell out, "It's a miracle! Her right chamber is there. It grew. It's there. Look, Cewanda. It's right there." But, that never happened. Every time she has a test, it's not there. Just those same three heart chambers. No fourth chamber.

So, I have to continue to believe that she can still live with only three chambers, day after day, week after week, year after year?

That's going to be enough for her body to sustain her life for years to come? Yep, I have to believe that. I have to believe Hebrews 11:1: *Now faith is the substance of things hoped for, the evidence of things not seen.* I have to believe that her heart is whole, despite the fact that my eyes are physically seeing three quarters of a heart. I have to see it as complete. Whole. With nothing missing. Nothing lacking.

Before she was born, I wouldn't allow myself to get attached to something that was going to be taken from me.

Wouldn't allow myself to love it. Couldn't smile through the pregnancy. For what? Smiling meant everything was okay, and it wasn't okay to me. Smiling meant I was happy about the circumstances, and I wasn't. I didn't want to talk about it. How could I have a joyful pregnancy and talk about a baby who was not going to survive? Just the concept sounded foolish to me. I couldn't even entertain the thought. I didn't think there was a chance of survival because that's what I was told. The doctors hadn't given me much hope for the baby's future, so I couldn't see beyond the doctors' reports. They knew more than I did, right? Surely. Of course they did, right? They're doctors, after all. Talk about a devastating shock to your system. To me, it felt like the quickest way to deem yourself mentally ill is to tell a mom that her child is going to be born to die. Wow. Straight jacket, here I come.

CHAPTER 3

BIG SISTER SYDNEY

So then, while we have opportunity, let us do good to all people, and especially to those who are of the household of faith.

Galatians 6:10

The doctors told us that the decision to continue the pregnancy would forever affect our relationships, finances, employment, and everything else we could and could not imagine. Sydney was fourteen years old at the time, already a very difficult age in a young girl's life. Then, she became a big sister, again. She was a sophomore in high school when she got the news, "We're having another baby."

She was like, "Really, mom? That's embarrassing."

She wasn't mad. She was mortified. She said that was disgusting for her mother to be pregnant because surely it was all about her and her image at that age. It's funny now that I look back on the day we told her. She had a grossed out look on her face that said she didn't want to picture the circumstances that took place to lead up to her mother being pregnant. No kid wants to have a visual of that.

She was fine with it eventually, but then we got the news that her new brother or sister had a heart condition. What does a teenage girl do with that information?

Keep it bottled up inside, of course, and not talk about it, like it's not happening. It made it easier for her so she wouldn't have to deal with it. She wouldn't have to hear me talk about it and cry. During the next few years, Kendall was in and out of the hospital. Sydney was pretty busy, so that was a relief for me that she was old enough to have school and other activities to occupy her time.

Fast-forward a couple of years to the day of Sydney's high school graduation party. Kendall was in the hospital, recovering from pneumonia. She had to have a thoracotomy, a surgery that relieves some of the air and fluid from the lungs. This incision was made across the left side of her back. I was so emotionally torn because we had been planning Sydney's graduation party, not knowing Kendall would be in the hospital at the time. How could I leave my baby in the hospital to go celebrate my oldest daughter's high school accomplishment? How could I go to the graduation party and smile, laugh, talk and eat cake while my three-year-old baby was in the hospital alone because all of our family was going to be at the party?

I had been talking about this for weeks with the nurses. They knew us so well by then that they agreed to take good care of Kendall for a few hours while I went to the party. I felt sick about it. It was kind of them to offer, but if it came down to it, of course I would've gone to the graduation party. As it turned out, I didn't have to make that decision with my head or my heart. The ICU doctor released Kendall from the hospital early the afternoon of the party! So, we all got to go to the party.

By the fall of 2012, I had an eighteen-year-old, seven-year-old and three-year-old. Sydney moved onto the university campus and started taking courses to become an RN. She thought that's what she wanted to do, but I think the memories of seeing her sister in the neonatal intensive care unit and pediatric ICU most of her short life scarred her perception of the joys of nursing. She didn't want anything to do with nursing. She couldn't handle it. I told her that her experiences with Kendall would probably make her an even better nurse because she would be more caring and empathetic, and could relate to the parents better. But she said, "Nope, can't do it." That was completely fine with me, as long as she found her passion.

She changed her major to Communications and I could tell this was her calling. She lived on campus the first two years and I rarely saw her, except at church a couple times a week. She was going to school full-time and working. I was so busy with Kendall that Sydney and I started having quick conversations and even shorter times together. I felt guilty once again because I couldn't spend time with her. On the weekends, she spent time with her friends.

Sometimes, I got angry because I felt like she should have spent that time at the hospital with me and Kendall. I couldn't understand why she never visited her little sister.

I started to think she didn't care about her sister, but neither of us brought it up. Before her junior year, Sydney moved back home to commute back and forth between college classes and work. We saw each other more because she was living at home and Kendall's hospital stays were shorter and less frequent. Four college years flew by and, next thing you know, it was time for Sydney's college graduation party. Where had the time gone? A college graduate with a Bachelor's degree in Communications and a minor in Criminal Justice. I was so proud of her. During Sydney's graduation speech, I found out a few things. I found out that she couldn't visit Kendall when she was in the hospital because she couldn't stand to see her baby sister hooked up to all those tubes and machines. I also found out that she admired Kendall. She called her the bravest girl she knew.

In her speech, she talked about how close she came to failing in school because she was so worried about Kendall and me. She had a hard time studying, staying focused and working. Here I was, thinking she was being selfish and didn't care, yet she was really scared and trying to get through this experience the best she could.

Before her junior year, I'd told her she couldn't stay on campus anymore. She needed to come home. We lived right down the street from the campus so that was money we could save on housing. I believe that was a good decision because she was able to focus more and we needed each other, in a sense. Even though there is a fifteen-year age difference between my girls, they really do love each other. Sydney even got **BeKendallStrong** tattooed on the inside of her arm (that's the only tattoo I was okay with). She is one of Kendall's biggest supporters and cheerleaders. I truly believe Kendall's journey has helped shape Sydney into a compassionate, determined, won't take no for an answer, yet strong young lady. We definitely could not have got through this without her being such an easy young adult to raise.

CHAPTER 4

BIG BROTHER QUENTIN

To godliness brotherly kindness,
and to brotherly kindness love.

2 Peter 1:7

Quentin, or "Quenny Quen Quen," as I like to call him, is our only son. Quentin was four years old when Kendall was born. Old enough to know he was a big brother, now he finally had someone he could be the boss of instead of being bossed around. However, he wasn't old enough to know what was really going on around him. Of course, I still felt guilty with him having to be shuffled back and forth to grandma's house, home, school and the hospital over the years.

My mom kept him busy enough after school and on the weekends, so he didn't really feel neglected and jealous of Kendall. I was glad about that. For the first few years, Kendall was in the hospital more often than not. So, when she was home, we held her a lot because we never really got that bonding experience at the hospital. When she started moving around, walking and getting into Quentin's things, I wouldn't let him take it back or play rough with her. He thought he should be able to tackle her and take his stuff back. He's a boy. He wanted to roughhouse her and protect his stuff. I felt like I always had to step in and save her. I wouldn't let him grab his things out of her hands, even though it clearly didn't belong to her. I was too afraid he would knock her down and she would get hurt, or that she would cry too long and turn blue. I am still very protective of her in that way.

Over time, Quentin saw this as Kendall getting away with stuff, even when she knew what she was doing. She knows I'm going to discipline him, not her, so she takes total advantage of it.

Even today, she's the ring leader of the sibling rivalry. The smallest and youngest is usually the culprit. So, one day, I had to back off and let Quentin handle the situation within reason to let her know she can't boss everybody around without consequences. Every time she does anything that she should get in trouble for, I holler out, "Kendall, show them your sad face." She shows Sydney and Quentin her pitiful, but cute face, in hopes that they will have mercy on her. As she got older, they stopped buying it though.

Now that Quentin is in middle school, that makes him feel a lot older than Kendall because he says she still goes to the baby school. But there's not a day that goes by that he doesn't run to open the door for her when she gets out of school and off of the bus. He watches the clock and every day, he is at the garage door at 3:45, waiting for his sister. Then, the fighting begins. But he loves his sister and he is her protector.

CHAPTER 5

PARENTING

*Show yourself in all respects to be a model of good works,
and in your teaching show integrity, dignity.*

Titus 2:7

Honesty is freeing. I used to think that my business is my business and nobody else's. Some things should remain private, but there are a lot of things that people go through that will help someone else. Someone else may be going through the same thing and be ashamed to talk about it because they fear they will be judged. After all, that's what people tend to do. We sit back and judge other people's lives based on what we think we would do if faced with such a situation. However, the fact of the matter is we could never walk in their shoes because we couldn't handle their situation. Nor would we want to if we ever knew the pain of the details of what they've had to live through.

When Kendall was first diagnosed with congenital heart

disease, my husband and I had been married for three years. Strong marriage. Two kids. Both of us worked full-time. Great incomes, cars, a home, good health. We had fun together, went out on dates and laughed a lot. Having this third and last child was going to make our commitment to each other and our family that much more solid and stronger. Once we knew about the heart diagnosis, one of the first few things we were told was that if we continued with the pregnancy, It would make our family life as we knew it more difficult, more strenuous and more challenging. At the time, we really didn't know what that meant. But we did know that if we ever got to that point, we would overcome whatever obstacle came our way because that's what we always did.

Only thing is we didn't really know what we were saying, "Yes" to. Overcome what? Overcome how?

Initially after Kendall was born, we were unbelievably strong. We had a system and, when we couldn't be with her around the clock at the same time, we had to start doing it in shifts according to a schedule. That was okay because we wanted to be the ones to be there with her. God fixed it so that I could take a leave from work while, at the same time, my husband got a promotion. So, finances were not an issue. Our bills were never behind. I was able to spend the majority of the day with Kendall at the hospital, leave the hospital to meet Quentin at home when the bus dropped him off in the afternoon, and spend the night at home. Damon worked from 6 a.m. to 4:30 p.m. Then, he'd go to the hospital Tuesday through Friday after work, spend the night at the hospital, and go to work from there.

After Quentin got on the bus in the morning, I would head down to the hospital again for the day. That pattern continued for weeks and months at a time over the years. One of us would make our overnight weekend stays on Friday and Saturday, and the other one on Sunday and Monday to give us a break from hospital food and sleeping in chairs. It also gave one of us more time to spend with Quentin and take care of household duties.

Our time together became less and less. We saw each other in passing as we exchanged Quentin in the hospital parking lot or in Kendall's hospital room on the weekends. We talked on the phone as he was leaving the hospital to go to work or as I was leaving home to go to the hospital. It was very easy for us to take all of our frustrations out on each other because, by now, we weren't even living together under one roof. One of us was always at the hospital. We became strangers.

As a nurse, I'm a nurturer by nature. Add being a nurse to having a child that needs someone to look after her 24/7, and I would say I was pretty much obsessed with Kendall. You would think it was a relief when she came home. Yes and no. Yes, because it was more convenient to not be running back and forth to the hospital. But no because of the constant physical closeness that I had to have with her, even at home. I knew her cues, her normal blue color versus her "get me back to the hospital blue" color.

I knew when she was feverish by the way she breathed, without having to check her temperature. She breathed hard and loud because of her narrow airway. I had to be on alert when she was breathing too loud or when I couldn't hear her breathing *at all*. Did that mean she was getting a break, and she was quiet and comfortable, or did that mean *she wasn't breathing*? I wasn't sleeping because I was always listening for her loud breathing—or no sound at all.

To say my husband and I were not on the same page was an understatement.

Because of my nursing background, I was like a human baby monitor. I wanted to just stare at her every minute of the day to make sure she was okay. I was consumed with her when she was asleep and when she was awake. If something happened to her, I thought I was the one who was supposed to be the first one to notice. People would blame me if something happened to her because, when people know you're a nurse, they expect you to know everything there is to know about something medical-related. My husband is very matter-of-fact. He more or less always gave me the, "Everything is fine. You need to relax," type of response. That came off to me that he was strong and I was weak. I was worrying for no reason. I wasn't as tough as he was.

I'm in no way implying that he doesn't love her as much as I do. We just communicate differently. I didn't want to be strong or tough. I just wanted to be Kendall's mom. I didn't want to be her nurse, but I ended up being both. I couldn't separate the two. There was no way to separate the two roles when you have this emotional attachment. We both love her, but men and women show it differently.

Love can bring you closer, but it can also cause distance. All of the time apart brings a strain on your relationship. Then, when you are together, your focus is on that child who needs you for everything. This causes you to put each other last. It hasn't been easy, but we've had to fight our way back to learning how to get to know each other again. We learned how to separate being married from being parents.

The husband/wife relationship is supposed to take priority over parenting. We are still working on this today to save our family unit. I finally did go back to work after a while because I needed to separate myself from Kendall for my mental health and sanity.

I had to separate myself from her day-to-day care, or I was going to lose it. Her doctors' appointments and procedures became less frequent, so I decided it was time to have some adult conversations and interactions.

I went back to work gradually. I started out working one day a week, then part-time, then finally back to full-time. This was a great big accomplishment for me because I never thought I would trust another human being enough to watch her as closely as I did. She had spent quite a while in physical, occupational and speech therapy. So, everyone at school, including all of the teachers, knew her.

The transition was easier than I thought.

That transition was easier because her only caregivers had been myself, my husband and my mother. We didn't trust anyone else to take care of her at home. They didn't know her normal vs. her abnormal cues that something was wrong. Because the therapists spent a lot of time at our home with her and at school, my mind was more at ease. They knew her well enough to know when to call me and/or 911.

That's how I gauged who could watch her. I always asked myself, "Will this person know when or if they need to call 911?" If not, I wouldn't leave her.

CHAPTER 6

BELIEVING

Then Jesus said, "Did I not tell you that if you believe,
you will receive the glory of God?"

John 11:40

To say I have been living a brokenhearted life is an understatement. I certainly didn't know that you could grieve something without there being an actual death. I found out that you can grieve the loss of an idea of something that you thought was going to be perfect. I was grieving the loss of the child who should have been born as healthy as the other two. It is really devastating to watch your child have surgeries and procedures, get blood transfusions, be in pain, see their scars and tears, put on a ventilator, then taken off the ventilator, and not be able to do anything to physically make all of it go away.

How was I supposed to be in faith that God was going to work it out? That Kendall would live and not die when, right before my eyes, she had several code blues. I would be lying if I said I wasn't scared then and even now. She's coded before, several times actually. So, what's to say her heart won't stop again? It's the same three quarters of a heart that she had when she was born.

Over the years, I have had to learn how to "walk by faith, not by sight." I can no longer live my life based on the reports I receive from the doctors.

I have to listen to the report and the recommendations they give, but I don't have to accept that report as the final say. I believe the Lord's report. I believe that Kendall will live and not die. I believe that everything they said about her quality of life is based purely on statistics, findings and past patient outcomes. I also believe she was born, lived and has survived for a purpose. A purpose that will qualify her to change what has already been written in medical books. She has changed conversations. Doctors will practice medicine differently based on something that has worked for her that they can now try on another baby and be successful. The name Kendall will mean something.

I will not allow others to tell her she can't do something because I know she has been created to do great things. When she gets tired or short of breath, instincts tell her to rest. She does, but she doesn't rest long. She's resilient. When I'm watching her do physical things that I know cause her to be short of breath, or turn pale or blue, I immediately want to make her stop and sit down. I'm thinking about the "what ifs" and what could happen next if her oxygen level gets too low. Most times, I will only tell her to be careful and rest if she needs to. I seldom tell her to stop doing anything she loves.

If you watch her long enough, you will see her doing whatever she is doing with a smile on her face, laughing, or trying to accomplish the task, with a look of determination on her face. That smile makes my heart melt. I think back to all of the times she couldn't smile because of pain and tubes. Our pastor has taught us many things over the years, but the main thing that got us through this was *faith*. Faith as we knew it pre-Kendall was not sufficient. This was going to take some next-level, supernatural faith. The support, prayers and love that people showered us with was something we had never experienced before and we welcomed it.

Faith is such an individual gift. You can't live off of somebody else's faith. It's one of those things that you don't know how much you have until you have to put it to use. Wow. We have had to pray like we never have before.

I thought I knew God and had a solid relationship with Him. Thought I trusted Him. What I needed God for at this time was going to take more than the itty bitty faith I had been walking around with. I got there eventually. Through a lot of prayer, patience and allowing God to put us in situations where we had to depend on Him, I now know Him as a healer, a provider, a comforter and a sustainer.

I'm not going to say that I have mastered this thing.

I'm still human and, when it comes to my kids, I surely get tested on how I'm going to react. I have come a long way. I am still a work in progress, but my faith in miracles that only God can perform were witnessed right before my very own eyes. I don't believe in His power because of what someone told me or something I heard. I witnessed God perform a miracle right before my own eyes.

CHAPTER 7

LORD, I BELIEVE!
BUT HELP MY UNBELIEF

Because of the littleness of your faith; for truly I say to you, if you have faith the size of a mustard seed, you will say to this mountain, 'Move from here to there,' and it will move, and nothing will be impossible to you.

Matthew 17:20

That whole process of staying in the hospital, eating whatever food was available, not sleeping, and literally sitting and looking at monitors that beeped, dinged, alarmed and literally made you want to throw all of it out the window, was my new normal. I was completely sad, depressed and constantly crying. I didn't want anyone to come to the hospital to visit. I started eating more and more unhealthy food, sitting and staring into space.

I had a hard time picturing Kendall's future. My mind kept replaying horrible images because I still didn't know how long she would live. I wanted her to live, but I honestly didn't know if she would or not. In fact, I begged her to keep living. But honestly, I was so scared that she would die. That's why, as I said earlier, I was grieving. I was a nervous wreck. Anytime I went to the store, I pictured that the ambulance would be at my house when I turned the corner on my street. That was no way for me to live. I didn't want to think that way. But the devil brought those thoughts to my mind and, unfortunately, I let those scenarios play out to see what would happen. It was never a good ending.

We don't have to let those horrible thoughts play out in our heads. I didn't know I had the power and authority over my own thoughts to snap myself out of it and think positive, even in the most horrible situation.

I was praying that Kendall lived. Everyone I knew, and even people I didn't know, were praying that she had a full recovery. In spite of all of that, I didn't fully believe that she would pull through and, if she did, I wondered what kind of life she would have. I believed God worked miracles, but deep down, I thought He only worked them out for everyone else. Would He work one out for me? I wasn't sure. When the Bible says, "Walk by faith," that's exactly what it means. You can't see faith. It's not something that's visible. Either you have it or you don't.

I had to have the kind of faith in God that I had when I prayed for someone else's situation. The same God who gave miracles to others was the same God who was going to perform a miracle for me. I had to trust Him totally and completely. After all, Kendall was His child *first*. He lovingly entrusted her to me on this earth to be her mother, but she was His, *not mine*. He loved me enough to allow this precious little girl to be my daughter. He was going to allow me to enjoy her, raise her, teach her, love her and be blessed by her life. That's when it clicked.

I couldn't let the devil have Kendall. She was a gift to me and he was not getting my baby. I didn't have to entertain anymore thoughts or scenarios of her dying. I had to speak life over her and find Scriptures that would match my new confessions I was going to speak and pray over her. He (the devil) has no power or authority. This is how I started to build up my faith. I started believing the opposite of what the devil said to me. I had to speak Hebrews 11:1 at all times: *Now faith is the substance of things hoped for, the evidence of things not seen.* I was still looking for a miracle of healing, but the part I was missing was that she was already a miracle. She was already healed. I believed that to be true, but I had to put it to use. I had to believe I saw her heart whole, not three quarters, but whole. I had to see her as a healed little girl, with all organs and blood vessels in her body working perfectly, even when all the test results showed the opposite.

CHAPTER 8

THE 20TH

Set your minds on things above, not on earthly things.

Colossians 3:2

Over the first few years, Kendall was in and out of the ICU too many times to count. She had her fourth open-heart surgery on December 10, 2012. The final surgery. Completion surgery. The Fontan procedure was the final surgery to complete the series. There are no more shunts or artificial equipment inside of her heart. It is functioning. We are praying that it continues to function and support her body, and all of her organs function without needing a transplant. Sometimes I pray for a new heart, but without all of the complications.

But most of all, I pray to God that He makes the one she has function as whole and brand new. Everything went well with the surgery itself and she was recovering nicely, except she had some fluid around her left lung. After many X-rays, chest tubes and tests, it was determined that she would have a bronchoscopy (remove fluid from around the lung). December 20th was the day of that procedure. The anesthesia doctors came to the room to get her and allowed Damon to carry her instead of her going on a cart to the operating room.

As we walked down the hallway, she threw up all over the floor and all over my husband's shirt.

I had an eerie feeling, but I shook it off as nervousness. I simply wanted her not to need any more procedures. After the procedure, they brought her back to her room. We walked in and they told us to go back to the waiting room because she had coughed out her ventilator tube and they had to put it back in. I remember crying and shaking my head all the way there. I was just so sad that she had to go through so much. I wanted this to be over.

We were in the waiting room quite a while. I got another eerie feeling and I knew something was wrong. We had been in the waiting room plenty of times, so I knew how long it usually took for them to call us back to her hospital room. My stomach was in knots. I started crying again. When I looked up, I saw two of the cardiac nurses coming our way with a look of horror and disbelief. I started screaming, "No! No! No! No! No," as they got closer to us.

One of them told us that the doctors were doing all that they could do. I hate those words.

They walked with us back toward the room. It felt like time stood still. I had an out-of-body experience because I wanted to see Kendall. Then again, I didn't because that would make it too real. What I saw next continues to play in my head over and over again, even today. The doctor was doing chest compressions on my three-year-old baby. That is not anything you ever want to witness. I wouldn't wish that on anybody. I looked at the monitor, which had no reading. I looked at the many people in the room. I looked at the bags of IV fluid and medicine being pushed through her veins, the people running in and out of the room. They put IVs in both her legs. People stared at us and I stared back. Everybody moved so quickly, working and looking at us at the same time. I remember pacing, screaming, crying the whole time.

As I got to the bottom of the bed, I got a better look at her. While she was getting the chest compressions, blood was coming out of the incision in her chest from her open-heart surgery she had ten days prior. It wasn't healed yet, so the compressions made it ooze blood. It was horrifying. I begged them to save her. The nurse was saying, "Come on! Let's go. They're doing all they can." I didn't want to go, but I didn't want to stay, either. It was too hard to watch, but I didn't want to *not* be there. So, we went as far as the outside of the door. We watched the monitor go from heartbeat to no heart beat. Low heartbeat to no heartbeat.

They gave my husband and I chairs so we could sit. We gave the nurse phone numbers to call our parents and our pastor. The chaplain came and waited with us. At this point, I don't think I made a sound. I just stared inside the room, watching them work, hoping I would wake up from this bad dream. The doctor who was in charge of the code blue came out and kneeled down in front of us, giving us the details of what happened.

It felt like time stopped. I didn't know if the cardiac arrest was ten minutes or two hours.

So, I asked him how long he worked on her. He looked on a clipboard and said forty-five minutes. He looked surprised by his answer, too. He said that he saw one of Kendall's fingers move during the CPR and that's the reason he kept going. Wow. A move of a finger. Thank God he saw that. Our mothers came that night. Our pastor and church family came that night. We prayed and prayed and prayed.

They allowed us to gather in a conference room. We took turns going back and forth to the room to be with Kendall. Our good friend came up to be with us. He had on a shirt with a t-shirt underneath. He literally took off the top shirt and gave it to my husband to put on because he was still wearing the shirt that Kendall had thrown up on before her procedure. He literally gave him the shirt off of his back. I will also never forget how our church family came and changed the atmosphere. We felt supported and we were reminded that we were supposed to have faith in the good times and the bad. This was not the time to lose hope, talk negatively and worry. This was the time to trust God. This was when my faith walk truly began. Thursday, December 20, 2012 at 7:00 p.m.

Kendall suffered a cardiac arrest that day. She also had a stroke as a result of the lack of blood flow to the brain. She lost all ability to sit, stand, walk and talk. She went through extensive physical, occupational and speech rehabilitation inpatient and outpatient over the next few years. Gradually, over time, she has regained most of what she lost due to her brain injury. Today, she is a very happy, loving and active nine-year-old. She amazes all of the hospital staff and teachers who have worked with her. No one thought she would be where she is today. But God knew.

She continues to work hard. She doesn't like to be told she *can't* do something. She is so strong and her life is such a testimony to others that if she can overcome everything she has been through, they can, too.

Children are so resilient. They recover from things that adults would not be able to survive.

She has residual effects from the stroke that I guess I don't even see until I see someone stare or boldly ask, "Why does she breathe like that? Does she have asthma?" Everything about her is so normal to me now that I don't see the left-sided weakness, the pauses in her sentences to breathe, or her smile that's sometimes uneven.

For years, on the 20th of every month, I had flashbacks and was sick to my stomach. I wept and reminded people that the 20th was the day that I thought I'd lost her. I thought I was supposed to be sad the 20th of every month, especially every December 20th. The truth is nobody remembered the date except me. I tortured myself. I gave that date too much credit. The details of it are still very clear to me. It was a Thursday evening around 7 p.m. It was during a shift change for the nurses and the doctors were rounding outside of her room at the room next door. That was no coincidence. The doctors were right outside her door. Everybody that God wanted to be there was there.

When God reached down and brought her back to life, He saved my life, as well. Now when I find myself dwelling on that horrific visual of the CPR, I purposefully shift my mind to see the progression she has made from that day until now. Then, there was no movement, very little impaired speech, no smiles and no recognition of who anyone was. Now there is full mobility. She is full of life and has no impaired speech. She has no portable oxygen and no home monitors.

CHAPTER 9

SCARS ARE A TESTIMONY

I praise you, for I am fearfully and wonderfully made.
Wonderful are your works; my soul knows it very well.

Psalm 139:14

I would be telling the biggest lie if I said twenty-four hours a day, seven days a week, I was a smiling, walking, talking PSA or billboard for all mothers of children with a medical challenge. That is far from my reality. But what I can say is that I have come a long way.

It's a process. I'm not consumed with her like I used to be. I still keep a careful eye out, like any parent would, but I have to let her live a normal life. I have to live one, too. She has to be able to do what other children her age do. After all, she has a voice and she can let us know when she needs to take a rest. I live every day expecting her to have a better day than she did before. When any scary moment comes up and she looks a little pale, or she's breathing a little harder, or her feet and hands look blue, I pray and don't panic. We just keep it moving. No bringing out the monitor and checking her oxygen level every time I think she needs it, like I used to. Instead, I keep calm and remember how far she's come. I allow her to have fun.

Children often only panic in a situation when we make a big deal out of it. She doesn't remember any details about the things that have happened to her, and that is a good thing. She's just now starting to ask about all of the scars on her chest. Her scars are her testimony to others about her journey.

I took her to a dermatologist because I thought maybe we could get some fading cream. The doctor said it was not that simple. Since she had several surgeries in the same area, and now has keloids, the only thing he could do was give her injections and cut away the keloid areas. We declined.

She's been through too much to now add cosmetic surgery to her list. So, we don't allow the scars to dictate anything negative to her.

If she brings it up, we remind her that she has a story behind those scars and that she is beautiful. When she doesn't make a big deal about them, we don't either. We don't allow her to concentrate on them. The only attention they will get is if we are giving a testimony about what she's been through.

CHAPTER 10

NEVER ALONE

Even though I walk through the darkest valley, I will fear no evil, for you are with me, your rod and your staff, they comfort me.

Psalm 23:4

I didn't take advantage of the support groups that were made available to me. I wish I had. I didn't because I thought surely, I didn't have time to go to any group meetings or chat online. I also thought that no one could relate, even if they were going through the same thing. I thought for sure our case was special, unique, different and worse than anyone else's. What I know now is that bonding with other people who are going through a similar situation helps to validate your grief, your feelings and your journey.

Who am I to say that if someone's child has asthma or Leukemia that Kendall's diagnosis trumps theirs? It doesn't matter what your child has been diagnosed with, as parents, we all feel the same helplessness. We all want our child to be healed and not suffer another day. Many days, I went to the hospital and saw a child on a portable ventilator in the lobby. I saw the child with a bald head and a mask on, fighting cancer. I saw the child in a wheelchair with a disability that has left him or her unable to walk and/or talk.

That's when I have to give God thanks.

I still have to thank Him that Kendall is fully functional and not dependent on any machines to keep her alive. She has to take medication every day, but there was a time when she had to receive that medication in a feeding tube. The fact that she can take them on her own with a spoon, or even chew them, is a victory. God is good. Doctors' appointments have been yearly now instead of every three to six months. We are down to four doctors altogether. That is truly a big accomplishment.

Kendall is a fourth-grader who is very determined to keep up with her peers. She has some physical limitations with her hands as a result of the stroke. Her sensation in them is decreased so, although she doesn't write as fast as the other children, she's still come a long way. It's not a competition as far as we are concerned. A few years ago, she couldn't even sit up or speak, let alone hold a pencil in her hand. The race is not given to the swift, but to the one who endures until the end. Kendall will finish her course. Of that, I am sure.

CHAPTER 11

FROM BROKENHEARTED TO BLESSED

The LORD is near to the brokenhearted
and saves those who are crushed in spirit.

Psalm 34:18

After many years passed, I met more families with similar stories. I wish I had known of other families' stories that could have given us hope. A few years ago, we were completely devastated and didn't know of any success stories of children who were doing well.

People ask all the time, "How is Kendall doing?" or "Is she all done with surgeries?" My answer to those questions is, "She is doing well and the doctors say, as she gets older, we will see if she needs a heart transplant." I don't think about that or worry about it. We take each day at a time.

I can't be consumed with thoughts about that type of

major surgery that may or may not happen. If she needs a new heart, at some point in her life, God will give her the best one He ever created. If she doesn't need a new one, He will strengthen the one she has and it will function just like a new one. I have to believe that. I don't believe in coincidences. I know that God knew exactly what He was doing when He allowed me to have a passion for nursing. Not only nursing, but I work in a High-Risk Antenatal Unit, which is a department that takes care of women who have high-risk pregnancies.

Some of these women have a diagnosis of a syndrome or defect for their babies. I am now able to talk to them on a personal, relatable level because I was in their shoes years ago.

I know what that news feels like. Now, I am able to tell them some information that will help them process the news. I can offer them some hope through our testimony. If you didn't have a test, you couldn't have a testimony, right?

I am writing this this book based on my perspective as a mother. Of course, Kendall has a father, who is very much a part of her life. He is the best dad she could have and they are very close. Many family members and close friends were there for us in so many ways. We love them for everything they have done for us. I certainly don't want this to seem like I did all the work singlehandedly. I am simply writing from a mother's heart. I needed to tell this story that has been bottled up inside of me since 2008 when we received the diagnosis.

I had no idea of everything that was involved with congenital heart disease. It was something I never thought I needed to know about. I simply wanted to tell Kendall's story. Our family's story. I wanted to bring awareness about this particular defect and give hope to those families who don't know anyone else who has ever gone through this. Now you do. There are survival stories that you need to know about when you feel like there is no hope.

I don't think people understand the numbness, sadness and depression that goes along with the daily care of a child who has any condition that requires most of your time, your energy, your thoughts, your hands. It drains basically every ounce of you. There's a mental shift that goes along with the blessing. It changes who you are. This child came into my life exactly when I needed. I didn't understand that at the time.

Now, I am more compassionate and sympathetic

toward other people who are going through a medical challenge, or even those who are taking care of someone who is medically challenged. It's not an easy job, but it is so worth it. I don't know what she will be when she grows up, but I know she will be someone that makes a difference in the lives of others. Together, we will educate people on congenital heart disease and they will be able to see a child who made it. She made it "through" and she is already a success story. She's going to make it. God doesn't make mistakes. There is some left-sided weakness and things she can't do right now. But she is getting stronger every day and will regain strength in the areas that were weakened.

Now, when I hear people say at children with disabilities slow, retarded, or ride the "short bus," it does something to me.

People use those words so freely and it really makes me angry. I don't like hearing them associated with any person, especially a child. I don't accept those words because they sound negative. I don't want her to ever feel singled out, different, isolated, made fun of or teased. I know it's not about what you're called, but it's more about what you answer to. That's what we will teach her.

I don't let statistics determine Kendall's future. Doctors have to tell you the worst case scenarios so that you can be educated and make the best decisions for your family. I am all for being informed, but it is a God thing for me. I know He has given Kendall the best medical care, treatment and staff possible to take care of her. I have no doubt about that. But I also know above all else, He is her healer. Medicine can treat her symptoms, but only God can heal her.

By faith, we will continue to love her and see her through all the phases that she goes through. We already know she is a walking miracle. We will all become stronger because of a little girl named Kendall. I'm so glad that God chose me to be her mother. He could've given her to anyone, but He chose me. He really loves me and I will do everything in my power to make sure she has the best life she can have. She has changed my life for the better.

Made in the USA
Middletown, DE
04 September 2019